LOW-COST LANDSCAPING

The Gardener's Collection

Better Homes and Gardens® Books

Des Moines

BETTER HOMES AND GARDENS® BOOKS
An Imprint of Meredith® Books

LOW-COST LANDSCAPING
Senior Editor: Marsha Jahns
Production Manager: Douglas Johnston

Vice President and Editorial Director: Elizabeth P. Rice
Executive Editor: Kay Sanders
Managing Editor: Christopher Cavanaugh
Art Director: Ernest Shelton

President, Book Group: Joseph J. Ward
Vice President, Retail Marketing: Jamie L. Martin
Vice President, Direct Marketing: Timothy Jarrell

MEREDITH CORPORATION
Chairman of the Executive Committee: E. T. Meredith III
Chairman of the Board and Chief Executive Officer: Jack D. Rehm
President and Chief Operating Officer: William T. Kerr

*All of us at Meredith® Books are dedicated to providing you with the
information and ideas you need to garden successfully. We guarantee
your satisfaction with this book for as long as you own it. If you have
any questions, comments, or suggestions, please write to us at:*

MEREDITH® BOOKS, Garden Books
Editorial Department, RW 240
1716 Locust St.
Des Moines, IA 50309-3023

Produced for Meredith Corporation by Storey Communications, Inc.,
Schoolhouse Road, Pownal, VT 05261
Editor: Gwen W. Steege
Production: Laurie Musick Wright
Writer: Pat Nichols
Photographers: PHOTO/NATS: Liz Ball, pages 27, 36, 41, 59; Gay
Bumgarner, pages 3, 25 (lilac), 32–33, 37, 47, 53, 56–57; Priscilla Connell,
cover, page 13; J. Eakes, page 35; Jennifer Graylock, pages 16–17; Don
Johnston, pages 48–49; Robert E. Lyons, pages 6–7, 39; Steve Paulson, page 23
(Mountain ash); Jennie Plumley, page 29; Ann Reilly, pages 21, 28, 51, 55;
David M. Stone, pages 15, 61, 63; Kim Todd, page 45; Virginia Twinam-Smith,
pages 9, 19; Marilyn Wood, page 43.
Illustrator: Brigita Fuhrmann

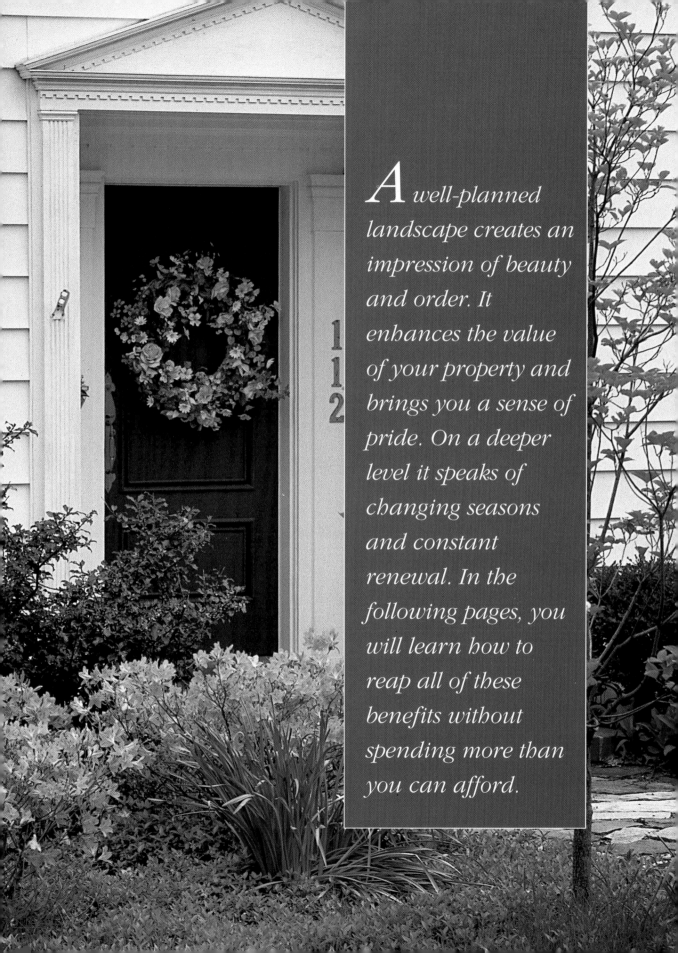

A well-planned landscape creates an impression of beauty and order. It enhances the value of your property and brings you a sense of pride. On a deeper level it speaks of changing seasons and constant renewal. In the following pages, you will learn how to reap all of these benefits without spending more than you can afford.

CONTENTS

Planning for Success 6

Low-Cost Plantings 16

Penny-Pinching Tips for Year-Round Care 32

Choosing and Caring for Equipment 48

Final Touches to Your Landscape 56

Index 64

Planning for Success

*T*wo guiding principles can save money on landscaping: keep it simple and do it yourself. Plan everything you want to do ahead of time, but don't be afraid to change if you find a better way as your gardens, lawn, and landscape plantings develop.

Begin with Ideas

Take time to plan carefully. You know what you like and what you can spend. Even with only vague ideas about how to go about it, you can develop a plan for an eye-catching landscape that will cost no more than you can afford. If you'd like to change an area, make a plan that encompasses your whole yard.

Start small. Instead of hoping to accomplish everything at once, start small. Determine the maximum you want to spend the first year. Costs are more manageable when spread over several years.

Try to visualize the yard once plants and trees reach maturity, not the way it looks when you put in young plants.

Take a walk around your property. Even if you start with no lawn or plantings in place, you need to walk around to get a feel for the way your land looks from different perspectives. As you explore, study the entire area, including flower beds, trees, shrubs, water conditions, runoffs, sunny and shady areas, desirable views—and undesirable views. Be sure to record elements you prefer not to accentuate, such as sheds, compost piles, even parts of neighbors' yards. Note the locations of utility poles and gas and electric meters.

Evaluate what you have. Do you have, or plan to create, outdoor living spaces, patios, pools, quiet corners for relaxation? What about existing gardens, both flower and vegetable? Do you expect to change their locations or just add or refine elements to make your landscape work better? Make lists of what you have and what you hope to have. At this point, don't worry if the lists grow long. Note

Gardener's Tip

As your plan grows more precise, look for inexpensive alternatives to the more costly projects—or reassess their importance.

anything, even if it appears too expensive to contemplate.

Focal points. Well-planned landscapes have one or more focal points: a tree, a view, a bench that draws you into the scene. Do any exist? Where might you put a focal point?

Look at the lawn. Does your lawn need a lot of work or just some improvement? Do you want a lush green lawn, an easier-to-maintain ground cover, or even raked gravel?

Consider how you use your yard. Do you have pets or children or both? Do you entertain often, or rarely? Do you need outside eating areas? More storage? Are driveways and paths appropriately situated?

Be stylish. Decide what style suits you best. That style should also be appropriate for the house, the neighborhood, and the climate. Do you want a natural design or one with a more formal or structured look? Do you envision an old-fashioned cottage look, an oriental

Striking color combinations demonstrate a well-thought-out garden plan. Here apricot tulips and white pansies complement the vivid deep pink of the azaleas behind.

scheme, or a contemporary design? Do you prefer sharply defined flower beds or ones that appear seamless with the rest of the environment? Do you want flowers or shrubs or both? What kind of trees do you like?

Gardener's Tip

Be realistic. If your plan is too ambitious, you will have trouble meeting your goals.

Developing a Plan

Make a budget. Estimate how much money you can comfortably commit to your landscaping project. Consider how much you can accomplish on your own and how much help you need. If your time is limited or you really don't enjoy gardening, plan a landscape that cares for itself. If, on the other hand, you love to spend your weekends and evenings trimming, mowing, and feeding plants, plan more challenging plantings.

Keep records. Keep a running tally of your expenses, even slight ones. Note the dates of planting, the varieties used, the spacing between plants, and the weather conditions. Such records will remind you which varieties were most successful, where you might have gotten along with less, or when you should have planted a bit later.

Seek advice. Doing it yourself doesn't mean you must forsake advice or help. Sometimes the best way to streamline processes and cut costs is to ask someone who knows. Don't count out professional landscape planners because you think the expense is too great. Many homeowners are on tight budgets, and a thoughtful landscaper can help you create a cost-effective plan. Some nurseries and garden centers offer free design services. Sometimes they will help design a long-range plan, with ideas for adding plantings each year. Proper planning and design can save mistakes and money in the long run.

Go to college. If you live near a college that offers landscape design courses, call to see whether students are looking for opportunities to practice design. They may offer their services reasonably or for free.

Gardener's Tip

Carefully select plant material with an eye to its mature size. Place taller plants in the rear where they won't overshadow shorter associates.

Consult with a friend or neighbor whose landscaping you admire. Ask how they designed it. Note what you like (and dislike) about it.

Take measure. Put your plan on paper. On a piece of graph paper, draw a map of your property to scale (making one ¼-inch square equal 3 feet). Include the dimensions of the land, the house, driveways, paths, and any small buildings. Note outside water faucets and underground utility lines. Draw circles to indicate trees and their overhangs, locations of plantings, and existing gardens.

Overlay a piece of tracing paper on your plan and sketch in what you want to add or change. Or make cutouts of individual elements, and move the cutouts around on the drawing, trying out different locations and adjusting sizes. Question how well a change serves the overall design.

Sun or shade. As you decide on spots to place trees, shrubs, and gardens, be sure to consider the amount of sun, shade, and moisture

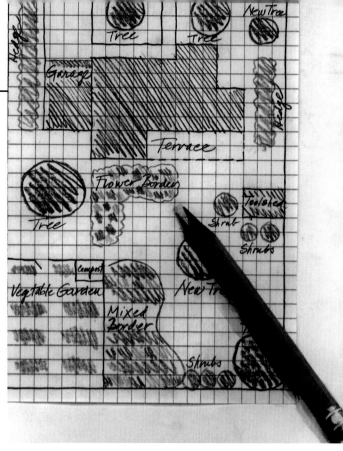

In order to visualize your landscaping assets and goals, draw a scale map of your entire property.

those locations receive, as well as the quality of the soil.

When your plan is complete, take it out to the yard and pace off the areas where you want to plant trees or shrubs or where gardens and paths will go. Mark off areas with hose or string and try to envision whether your paper plan will work.

Big Impressions for Little Money

Inexpensive, easy-to-do focal points can create big impressions. A focal point is an eye-catching feature, often one that creates an illusion of depth.

Simple arches suit any landscape style. Many inexpensive materials work well: PVC pipe, lattice, and saplings, for instance, are all effective, especially when covered with greenery. Pair an inexpensive arch with a bench, a garden, a statue, or even a container plant. Or, frame a special element with the arch.

Appreciate a view. If your landscape includes a view, frame it from both inside the house and outside. Plant a line of trees to draw the eye into the view. (Start with small plants; they do grow.)

Plant a garden with bright-colored annual flowers that can't be ignored. Start your own from seed, or save as much as 50 percent by waiting until the most concentrated spring selling season is over, then buying plants on sale. Bold annuals add pizzazz to any landscape. You'll get a bonus in no-cost flowers for summer bouquets.

Bench it. A garden bench is an attractive addition to a yard and provides a place to enjoy a closer look at the view you are creating. Look for good buys on replica park benches. If you catch a sale, you'll save even more.

Look to art. Know any aspiring artists or sculptors? You may be able to get an original wood or metal structure at very little cost, or perhaps even on loan. Or, haunt secondhand shops and garage sales with an open mind. Something

Gardener's Tip

A standard design scheme includes one tall plant, three medium, and five short. Plant the tall one slightly off center, group the medium plants together, then intersperse the small, ground-hugging plants among the others.

unusual or offbeat — and very inexpensive — could be a smashing success in your garden. When you visit garage sales look for cast-off architectural elements, such as old windows, door frames, or even railings, to use as whimsical touches in your yard.

Feature a rock. Do you have a big rock you can't get rid of? Use it as a focal point. Make it the beginning of a small planting that includes an inexpensive small birch tree, some spring bulbs, and colorful annuals.

Container plants. For high impact at low cost, use container plants at strategic places around the yard. Baskets, plastic or clay flowerpots, buckets, wooden crates, and boxes are all suitable and decorative containers for growing plants. Combine three or more color-coordinated plants for more interesting effects.

Reuse pots as much as possible. Ask others to save the pots in which their spring plants come.

Make a box. Construct a simple four- or six-sided wooden planting box at a fraction of the cost of buying one. Puncture several drainage holes in the bottom of a plastic tub and place it within the box to hold the soil.

Ready-mix concrete can be used by do-it-yourself gardeners in many money-saving ways. Follow the directions on the bag and mix as much or as little as you need in a wheelbarrow. Use it to make stepping stones or a bird bath.

Create an effective focal point on a small scale with a container water garden surrounded by container-grown annuals, like these gazanias, geraniums, petunias, sunflowers, and zinnias.

Cutting High-Cost Items

Saving in small ways is helpful, but finding ways to cut expenses on high-cost lawn and garden items can really affect your budget. Good secondhand equipment often serves well. Check classified ads, garage sales, and dealerships that take equipment in trade.

Lawn mowers. The cheapest mower is a push mower. It's quiet, there's no gasoline to buy, and you exercise when you use it. Keep your push-mower blades well sharpened and you'll find that they require less maintenance than power mowers and they don't break down as often.

If you buy a power mower, try to take advantage of end-of-season clearance sales. Purchase the best you can afford; a cheap mower often causes trouble in the long run. If it breaks down, repairs can be inconvenient and costly.

Riding mowers sit at the high end of the budget, but you don't need one unless you have at least ¼ acre to mow. Even then, you can do the lawn with a power mower—it just takes more time and effort.

Fertilizer spreaders, lawn rollers, rototillers, chain saws, and other heavy equipment may be needed only occasionally. Rather than purchasing any of these outright, rent one, buy it used, or get together with neighbors or friends and buy one for the group.

Patios and decks. As useful and handsome as these features are, they can be very costly. You will save a lot if you do most of the work yourself, look for inexpensive materials, and do the work in stages. Begin small and wait for another year to add extras, such as additional space, benches, and/or flower boxes.

Gardener's Tip

Plant sunflowers for the sheer pleasure of seeing such lovely big flowers growing in your landscape and also for the seeds that birds love.

Walkways. Create good-looking, serviceable paths with free or low-cost materials, such as shredded bark. (For more ideas, see pages 58–59.)

Trees and shrubs. Buy young, fast-growing trees and shrubs. Because they are less demanding in the nursery, these plantings cost less, yet they quickly grow to be handsome specimens on your property. Be sure to inquire about the plant's mature height and width, so that you choose one suitable for the location.

Watering systems. These not only make lawn and garden care easier, they use water more efficiently, creating big savings over time. Like other major investments, install these in sections over several years to spread out costs.

Erosion control. If your property is hilly, you may have to deal with erosion. Appropriate ground covers or vines are far less costly than the alternatives of terracing or building a retaining wall, which may involve

Spread costs over time by planning a simple deck that can be expanded by adding planters or even extra sections in future years.

not only expensive materials but also skilled labor.

Fencing. Purchase fencing in prebuilt sections and install it yourself. Check out the new plastic materials that look good, last longer than wood, and are maintenance-free in years to come. (For more ideas, see pages 60–61.)

Grass seed, fertilizer, and other lawn and garden supplies are less expensive when you buy in bulk. Look for end-of-season or other bargains for best buys.

Low-Cost Plantings

The trees and shrubs that grow in your yard are the backbone of your landscape. The lawn and other plantings are what hold it together. Trees provide solidity, shade, focal interest, even fruit. Shrubs visually draw different areas together; they grow quickly and add color and texture to your landscape. Lawns, ground covers, and other plantings supply the unifying elements that make it all work.

The Choice Is Yours

What kind of trees and shrubs you add to your landscape depends largely on what you want from them. Do you want shade, or protection from noise or wind? Do you want the sheer beauty of their shapes, or the splendid display of their flowers?

Native plants. Grow trees and shrubs that do well in your area. Many cost less to purchase because they are readily available. Plus, they'll require less water or fertilizer, and fewer insect controls or other plant-care products than exotic varieties. They are also more likely to survive and thrive for many years, and no costly replacements will be necessary. Inquire at a good local nursery for what is appropriate to your area.

Young plants. Save money by buying young plants. A large tree may be hundreds of dollars, while a smaller version costs considerably less. If you are patient, you may even purchase very young plants and keep them in a nursery bed where you can pamper them for a year or two until they are ready to be moved to permanent locations.

Save the trees. Sometimes tiny trees sprout in yards and gardens from seeds blown by the wind or carried by birds from a neighbor's property. Watch for these young seedlings in the lawn when mowing or in your gardens. Gently dig them out to plant them where needed or keep them in a nursery row for a few years.

Gather seeds when they drop from deciduous plants such as azaleas. Plant in moist peat moss and cover with a thin film of vermiculite in winter or spring. Once the days warm up, they should grow well. You may even see blooms the following year.

Gardener's Tip

Join a garden club. You will gather information and advice, and maybe share plants with other gardeners.

To maximize chances for the success of your plant investments, look for plants (such as this azalea) that are native or naturalized to your area.

Well-cared-for trees and shrubs, planted in the right places, grow quickly and thrive, once they establish themselves after the initial shock of planting. If you buy a small tree or shrub, expect a few years to pass before it settles in and begins to grow more rapidly. If you take care of your investment, fertilizing and watering it as needed, you will be rewarded for many years by a fine, healthy specimen.

Look for free or low-cost trees and shrubs offered by conservation, 4-H, or other organizations.

Fruit trees and bushes give you twice as much for the money: They provide shade and beauty, plus they bear fruit. Dwarf varieties take less space and bear at a younger age. Check with the nursery where you purchase them to learn how the blossoms are pollinated. You may need to plant two to ensure setting of fruit.

The Right Plant for the Right Place

Most trees do better in some locations than in others. Determine the amount of moisture you can provide, take account of your climate, consider winds and pollution from automobiles or industry, and test the kind of soil you have. Then, match the trees or shrubs you want with the conditions in your yard.

When you select a tree or shrub at a nursery, look for one with good color—no yellowing leaves or needles. Choose one with compact, sturdy growth. Plant it with care and provide plenty of water.

Choose a tree that will not over-scale your home. A very large tree, for instance, could dwarf a small ranch home. If you have a one-story house, a flowering tree such as a crab apple or dogwood may be a wise choice. For a two-story home, a larger tree such as a maple or oak may be appropriate. Cutting down your mistakes after several years is like throwing away hard-earned cash.

Gardener's Tip

Place an ornamental tree at least 15 feet from a house, a shade tree at least 25 feet. As the tree reaches its mature size, it needs adequate space so that it won't grow against the building.

Plant trees and shrubs yourself to avoid the extra charge for planting. Ask nursery personnel for directions and hints to make it easier. Dig a good-size hole, wider than the spread of the plant's roots. Mix a bucketful of compost with the soil that you removed from the hole. Set the plant at the same soil depth it grew in at the nursery. Fill the hole with soil and compost, taking care not to leave any air holes around the roots. Water thoroughly and keep the tree well watered, especially the first season: Give it as much as a bucket of water a day.

Choose foundation plantings that are in scale with your home. The pale yellow flowering scotch broom, dogwood, and azalea in this foundation planting will stay small, never overwhelming the house they frame.

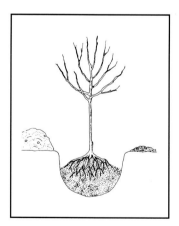

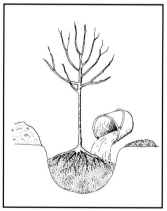

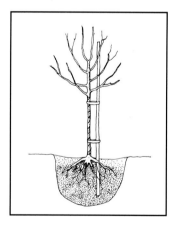

Prepare a hole wider than the spread of the plant's roots. Set the plant at the same depth it grew at the nursery. Replace the soil, taking care not to leave any air holes.

Water the plant well, both as you plant and for the entire planting season.

Stake the tree to keep it stable until roots provide a sure anchor for it.

Low-Cost Trees

The most popular trees used in landscaping remain familiar favorites. Evergreens such as spruces, Scotch pines, and Austrian pines are shapely and easy to maintain. Willows and silver maples are hardy and do well in wet areas.

Birches, are visually impressive because of their texture and pale bark. White or paper birches thrive in shade and grow 30 to 50 feet in height; their leaves turn yellow in the fall. Other birches include silver and weeping birches.

Honey locust, with its delicate, fernlike foliage, resists drought well. Not effective as a shade tree, it thrives in full sun.

Lombardy poplar works well in many low-budget plans because of its fast growth. It often grows 5 feet in a year, to a mature height of 70 feet. Look for growers who sell in quantity at lower prices.

Maple trees are welcome for their lovely change of color in the fall. Look for the popular red-leaved 'Crimson King' and the adaptable, drought-tolerant Norway maple.

Mountain ash grows as tall as 40 feet. In the spring it has showy white flowers, followed by red-orange or yellow berries through the summer until fall.

Oaks, with their commanding presence, evoke a sense of permanence. They grow quickly to a height of 60 to 80 feet. Plant in full sun in moist, well-drained, acidic soil.

Ornamental flowering trees, such as crab apple, cherry, dogwood, and magnolia, tend to remain small. Some won't do well in northern climates. If possible, look at the tree in bloom before you buy. Many crab apples are very inexpensive.

Pines tolerate dry soils, offer shade, and make excellent windbreaks. White pines grow quickly. The miniature mugho pine rarely grows taller than 3 feet. Austrian pine grows to about 50 feet.

Birch

Cherry

Honey locust

Maple

Mountain ash

Oak

Low-Cost Shrubs

A row of shrubs makes a good hedge, or plant shrubs individually or in small groups where you need their flowers, color, and texture. Shrubs also effectively shield unsightly conditions, block undesirable sounds, and provide windbreaks.

Shrubs, like trees, can be either deciduous or evergreen. Many flowering shrubs are hardy throughout the United States. The most common are likely to be the least expensive.

American bittersweet bears small, orange-capped red berries, much prized in the fall for dried arrangements. Let it ramble, or train it to climb a wall.

Arborvitae makes a good hedge that grows tall in a short time. Although not as dense as some hedges, arborvitae provides excellent screening very inexpensively.

Forsythia grows fast. Its bright, perky yellow flowers are one of the most welcome sights of early spring. Branches often arch to the ground, making forsythia a good candidate for layering to increase its numbers (see page 31).

Honeysuckle adds a sweet fragrance to your property. It likes full sun and moist, loamy soil. Its white, pink, red, or yellow flowers and fleshy berries attract birds.

Hydrangeas bloom all summer. Expect white flowers that turn green, pink, or rose as they age. Some varieties bear blue flowers when planted in acidic soil. Hydrangeas do well in full sun or very light shade. The flowers dry well.

Junipers take to pruning or shearing to form a hedge. A very popular plant that comes in many varieties, juniper grows easily, costs little, and likes hot, dry places.

Lilacs do well almost everywhere. Their showy lilac, white, and purple flowers are heavily scented.

Plant lilacs in full sun. Cut off the flower head after blooming to encourage increased flowering the following year.

Potentilla has single, roselike flowers in many colors that bloom from spring to fall. It likes full sun but tolerates partial shade, and needs little care once established.

Privet makes a fine dwarf formal hedge, and it is quite inexpensive. It has deep green oval or yellow leaves.

Rhododendron. Not all rhododendrons tolerate northern winters. If you choose to plant rhododendrons, buy from a local grower who stocks plants raised specifically for your area.

Spirea is an easy-to-maintain, inexpensive plant. It transplants easily. In sunny spots, it provides a bright display of color for several weeks in early summer. If you cut it back after bloom, it may flower again the same season.

Forsythia

Hydrangea

Juniper

Lilac

Rhododendron

Spirea

Low-Cost Lawns and Ground Covers

If trees and shrubs are the backbone of your landscape, lawns and ground covers hold it together.

A lawn usually costs less to install than a ground cover. Look for some of the older strains of grasses to ensure the most economical lawn. Make sure you get a mixture that is suitable for your climate and soil.

A ground cover may create the look you want better than grass, and ground covers usually involve less maintenance. In certain locations, such as under a very large shade tree, on a steep slope that is difficult to mow, or where water is scarce, ground covers solve a problem. Almost any low-growing plant can be used as a ground cover. In addition to the familiar pachysandra, ivy, and myrtle, for example, lily-of-the-valley and common violet are possibilities.

Wildflowers are another alternative to a traditional lawn. The attractively packaged canisters of seeds are rather expensive. Look for wildflower mixtures you can buy in bulk instead. Shop around.

For best results buy a mix suitable for your region and conditions. Don't expect to just scatter the seeds. Rent a sod cutter to remove grass from the area you wish to seed. If you prepare the soil well, expect to enjoy wildflowers for many years with little care and no additional expense.

Gardener's Tip

If you use a ground cover, buy it in flats of 100 plants. Individually potted ground-cover plants cost much more. One flat covers about 30 square feet.

Myrtle and lily-of-the-valley form a dense, lush green ground cover that thrives in partial shade and never requires mowing.

You can easily and inexpensively expand a ground cover of pachysandra by rooting tip cuttings. Cut pieces off the top of each plant, about 4 to 6 inches from the tip. Strip the foliage off the bottom portion of the stem. Dip each piece in a rooting hormone, insert them into soil mix in a small pot, and water well. Cover the plants with clear plastic and keep them moist. When roots begin to form, poke small holes in the plastic to increase the air supply.

Low-Cost Container Gardens

Growing plants in containers is a great way to get big effects for little cost and effort. Group containers at doorways or on patios and decks, position them in gardens after spring bulbs or early summer perennials have completed their bloom, or tuck them around foundation plantings for bright spots of color.

Choosing containers. Clay pots are classic and inexpensive. They are also porous, which means that air circulates to plant roots, but also that soil tends to dry out more quickly than it does in plastic pots.

Plastic pots are easy to clean and inexpensive. If you use them for heavy plants, weight them with stones in the bottom to keep them from tipping. For suggestions for recycled pots, see pages 44–45.

Soil for container plants. If you have only a few container plants, buy premixed soil. As with fertilizers and other plant supplies, soil mix is cheaper when purchased in quantity. To save even more, mix your own by combining equal parts of peat moss (or compost), vermiculite, and perlite. Do not use garden soil, which often drains poorly in containers.

Fertilizing container plants. Use an all-purpose, easily dissolved plant food for most container plants. Mix fertilizer at half strength and apply every two weeks.

An instant garden lines the front steps: marigolds, chrysanthemums, pansies, zinnias, and daisies.

Designing a planting. It's fun to create different combinations of plants for container gardens. The only rule is that each plant in a container requires the same amount of water, fertilizer, and light as the others. The possibilities for planting are endless. You can change your entire landscape mood and color scheme with little effort or cost.

■ Create a warm bright spot of color with yellow begonias, orange marigolds, and magenta impatiens.

■ Welcome spring with a planting of hyacinths and daffodils.

■ Make a salad planter with cool green parsley, a ruffled lettuce, some chives, and trailing thyme. You'll appreciate the textural interest in this planting, as well as its functional use.

■ Whites and pale colors show up well against dark foundation plants and in areas visible in the evening. Use white and pink petunias and gray-leaved trailing helichrysum.

■ Cacti and succulents are among the easiest-care plants, needing only weekly watering even in hot weather.

Welcome spring with container-grown paperwhites, alyssum, pansies, and petunias.

Gardener's Tip

Don't throw away old pots just because of salt and mineral buildup on the outside. Clean them by scrubbing, then dipping them in a mixture of 1 cup bleach to 1 gallon water, rinse well, and allow to stand for three days before planting.

Grow Your Own

Learn how to start your own plants from seed, cuttings, layering, and division. You'll have an abundance of plants at little or no cost.

Start your own flower seedlings, both annuals and perennials, indoors or in a special bed. Use them to enliven foundation plantings and shrub beds with their bright colors. You will save money over purchased plants, and have greater variety to choose from. Look for disease-resistant varieties, and you will also spend less on pesticides.

Take cuttings from your own plants or from those of friends and relatives. For best results, take cuttings of new growth from shrubs and trees in late spring. Use a sharp knife or pruning shears to cut 4- to 6-inch pieces from the ends of healthy branches. Make angled cuts. Dip ends in rooting hormone and plant the pieces in a 4-inch-deep mixture of peat moss, or ½ sand and ½ peat moss, or ½ sand and ½ vermiculite. Use a container with good drainage. Cover the

To start plants from cuttings, cut a 4- to 6-inch piece from the end of a branch.

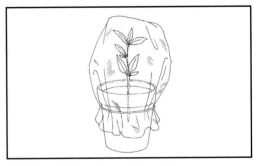

Dip cut end in rooting hormone, place in planting mixture, and cover the pot with plastic.

container with plastic and keep the soil mix damp. Place in bright, but not direct, sunlight. Once roots form (in one or two months), put the plants in pots. Wait until the following spring to move to the garden. Shrubs easy to propagate by this method include potentilla, euonymus, and evergreen azalea.

Learn to layer. Some plants are easy to start by a technique called layering. Lay a lower stem of the plant along the ground. Hold it close to the soil with a rock or brick, in several places if necessary. Mound a bit of soil over the stem at the point where it touches the ground and it will take root. If you begin this procedure in the spring, you probably can cut the rooted stock from the mother plant and replant it in the fall. Holly, juniper, euonymus, forsythia, privet, and lilac are all good candidates for layering.

Division. Lilacs, spireas, and evergreen azaleas, among others, are easy to divide in order to make a dense hedge. Look for 1-foot-tall "suckers"—stems that grow near the original plant. Cut a circle in the ground around a sucker, severing it from the main plant. Dig up the small plant carefully. Be sure to bring up all its deep roots. Replant in a new location and keep the young plant moist at all times. If you plant lilacs, enjoy both the

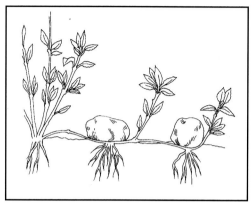

To start plants by layering, anchor branches along the soil until roots form.

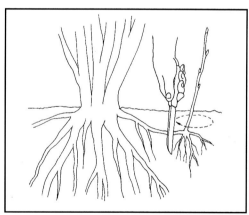

To start plants by division, cut "suckers" from the mother plant.

privacy of your "free" hedge and the wonderful aroma of the blossoms.

*W*elcoming landscapes need a certain amount of care — watering, pruning, and fertilizing, for instance. Learn the basics, find the least expensive way to accomplish the chores, then relax and enjoy the fruits of your labors.

Precious Water

That outside faucet that waters the gardens and lawn also runs up the water bill. An element crucial to keeping plants healthy and growing, water costs money in areas where meters keep track. Here are some ways to save.

■ Install a watering system. A drip system consists of water lines laid along shrub and flower beds, with nozzles directed at individual plants. Such a delivery system is very efficient because the water flows directly to the root system of each plant. A soaker hose, another watering system, is made of a porous material that allows water to seep through it along its entire length. Bury the hose just under the soil surface. When water runs through the hose, it saturates the soil in the area.

■ Make your own watering system using old hoses. Punch small holes along a length of hose, close off the end away from the faucet, and settle the hose into the garden. Run the faucet slowly to water the area.

■ Make individual drip waterers from empty plastic gallon jugs.

Poke a small hole near the edge at the bottom of each jug. Tuck the jugs beside shrubs or other plantings that need extra moisture, and fill the jugs with water from a hose as needed. Water will drip slowly from the hole right to the roots.

■ Collect and save rainwater. Use rainwater to water plants. Any large containers, such as garbage cans, barrels, or children's wading pools, will hold the water until you need it. (Don't allow saved water to sit too long, or it could turn stagnant and invite mosquitoes.)

■ Choose drought-resistant grasses, shrubs, and trees for your yard. (See pages 36–37 for suggestions.)

■ Mulch gardens with wood chips or sawdust to conserve water. Even grass clippings help. If you use black plastic, disguise it with a layer of grass clippings or other natural material.

■ Allow grass clippings to remain on the grass when you mow. They decompose, adding organic matter to the soil, which in turn helps the lawn retain and use water.

A drip watering system allows you to direct water right to the plant roots.

■ Where drought is a serious problem, replace parts of your lawn with usable areas of stone, wood, or gravel. Use porous stone, when possible, to allow rainwater to seep through to the ground.

Gardener's Tip

If you think a purchased water system would benefit your landscaping, install it in sections over several years to avoid a heavy expense in any one year.

Low-Water-Use Plants

When you are choosing plantings for your yard, consider how much water they require. Some take much less than others. Start with the suggestions listed on these pages and ask at a local nursery what plants are most appropriate in your area.

Creeping junipers tolerate dry conditions.

LOW–WATER–USE ANNUALS AND PERENNIALS
Belladonna
Coreopsis
Cosmos
Evening primrose
Flax
Gaillardia
Gayfeather
Iris
Mexican sunflower
Sedum

Save the cost of watering by choosing plants that tolerate dry soils.

LOW–WATER–USE SHRUBS

Cotoneaster
Elaeagnus
Euonymus
Juniper
Leadplant
Mountain mahogany
Nanking cherry
Rose
Saltbush
Yucca

LOW–WATER–USE GRASSES

Blue fescue
Blue grama
Bluestem
Buffalo grass
Eulalia grass
Fountain grass
Giant reed
Plume grass
Smooth brome
Tall fescue

LOW–WATER–USE TREES

Cedar
Elm
Golden raintree
Hackberry
Linden
Locust
Oak
Osage orange
Pine
Silk tree

LOW–WATER–USE GROUND COVERS

Bearberry
Cotoneaster
Coyote brush
Evening primrose
Gazania
Horseshoe vetch
Juniper
Santolina
Snow-in-summer
Verbena

Feed Your Garden for Less

Fertilizers can be an expensive item in a landscaping budget, yet they are important to the health of plants. Here's how to save:

■ Save money by buying fertilizers on sale, perhaps at the end of the season. Be sure to take advantage of coupons and rebates.

■ Buy as much as you can. It saves money to buy in quantity. Get together with neighbors and buy in bulk to save even more.

■ Cut your need for commercial fertilizers by making use of more organic materials: manure, compost, and wood ashes, for example.

■ Use a cover crop on your vegetable garden. Sow rye, oats, or field grass in the fall, then turn it under in the spring, adding nutrients to the soil.

■ Never waste grass clippings. A year's worth left in place equals the nutrients gained from two applications of lawn fertilizer.

Compost. One of the best ways to enrich and improve your soil is by adding compost to it. Compost is decomposed organic material that not only adds nutrients to the soil, but also improves the soil's texture. With added compost, sandy soils retain water better, and clay soils take on a lighter texture. Compost contributes dramatically to the quality of your gardens and landscape. Furthermore, it's easy and it's cost-free. The idea is simple: Pile up your organic castoffs—kitchen peelings, coffee grounds, eggshells (no meat products), grass clippings, faded flowers, leaves, sawdust, and small twigs. Occasionally add some soil, lime, and/or manure, if desired.

Gardener's Tip

Keep a plastic container by your sink. Instead of spending money on electricity to grind up garbage, slip castoffs into the container. At the end of the day, deposit the contents on the compost heap.

A simple-to-construct bin contains the compost that dramatically improves and enriches all soils.

Leave the compost pile alone for a few months. You can sprinkle it with water if it seems dry or turn it occasionally if you wish, but that's not essential. In time you will find the garbage has turned into a deep-colored, crumbly substance that resembles good soil.

Make a bin from chicken wire or wood slats if you want to enclose the compost pile.

If you generate a lot of organic refuse and need a quantity of compost, you may decide to create three piles. A three-section system built of wood, wire, or concrete blocks is convenient and inexpensive to set up. When the first section fills up, start filling the second, and then the third. Use the compost in rotation.

Spread the compost on top of the soil in the garden and around foundation plantings in the fall and dig it under. Notice the improvement when you work in the yard the following spring.

Gardener's Tip

Local energy-conservation groups sometimes offer good-quality plastic compost bins for very little money.

Save Two Ways with Mulch

Mulch means money saved. It conserves water by helping soil absorb all available rainfall and then slowing water evaporation from the soil. Mulch also makes foundation beds and gardens look better. Because it suppresses weeds, you'll spend less time on that landscaping chore. You can buy mulch material, but why spend money when so much mulch comes free? The secret to free or inexpensive mulching: Use whatever is available in your area.

■ Hardwood-bark mulch or sawdust may be available in quantity from local lumberyards or mills. They usually sell it very reasonably. Expect to pick it up yourself. Take along a shovel and some clean, empty trash barrels to put the mulch in.

■ Shredded brush is a by-product of utility and tree-cutting company projects. If they shred the brush cut from around pipes and wires, they may make it available to gardeners. Call for sources in your area. Tree companies usually offer the material free if the gardener picks it up. Some even help load it or deliver it to your home for a small fee.

■ Seaweed for gardeners who live near the ocean makes excellent mulch.

■ Grass clippings from your own and neighbors' lawns work well. Because clippings tend to heat when they begin to decompose, leave space around plants when you use them as mulch, or they may burn plants.

Gardener's Tip

When you get material from a brush-cutting operation, ask what you are getting. It may not be as attractive as you want. During summer months, for instance, it may contain green leaves and larger twigs, depending on the size of the chipper used.

■ Hay makes good mulch. At less cost than top-quality feed, you can often buy hay that is inferior for livestock, but still fine for mulch.

■ Packing material such as shredded newspaper, computer paper, or padded brown paper from stores and local businesses is good to use as mulch.

■ Fallen leaves are fine for the garden. They decompose quickly and add nutrients. When you rake leaves in the autumn, run the lawn mower over the gathered leaves to chew them up.

■ Pine needles make good mulch, especially if you grow plants that need an acidic soil.

Pine needles make a neat, no-cost mulch around pittosporum, cutleaf red-leaf maple, and azalea.

A Clean, Healthy Landscape

If you grow anything, sooner or later you learn about the insects and diseases that sometimes affect your lawn and plantings. The best way to keep insect damage to a minimum is to keep your property clean.

■ Remove insect pests when you see them.

■ Deadhead spent flowers and add them to the compost pile. Bugs find decaying, faded flowers delicious. After nibbling on them, they may move on to foliage or other flowers, doing further damage and sometimes spreading disease from one plant to another.

■ Clean up diseased leaves and branches and remove them and all plant refuse from your yard.

Gardener's Tip

Always strain a homemade spray several times through cheesecloth or very fine screening. If you don't, the solution tends to clog the sprayer.

Homemade controls. If you have an insect infestation, you can make one of the following inexpensive homemade sprays to remedy the problem.

■ Make a soap spray with 2 or 3 tablespoons of soap to 1 gallon of water. (Use a soap, not a detergent.) It should be safe to spray this directly on a plant, but it is a good precaution to test a small area, then wait a day or so before spraying the entire plant.

■ Hit soft-bodied insects such as mealybugs, whiteflies, and aphids with a hot-pepper-and-garlic spray. Make this effective spray by grinding hot peppers and garlic cloves with 2 cups of water in a blender. (Or use 1 tablespoon of garlic powder, 1 or 2 tablespoons of hot sauce, a few drops of liquid detergent, and 2 cups of water.) Spray the mixture on the plants. If you grow your own hot peppers, this spray will be nearly cost-free.

■ Try a mixture of 1 part water to 1 part vinegar as a spray to combat slugs.

Hand-picking insects works, and it doesn't cost a penny. Place dead bugs in a can with a soapy solution. Deter additional infestations by leaving the can near the plants the bugs savor.

Save aluminum pie plates and string them around the garden on poles to keep birds away from your berries.

Use certain flowers and herbs to deter insects. Marigolds, for instance, deter many insects. Tansy helps keep Japanese beetles away.

Make your own sticky traps to ensnare certain pests. Trap flying insects by spreading a mixture of equal parts of resin, turpentine, and castor oil on bright-colored disks or bowls. Hang the traps in and around the target plants.

Encourage birds to live in your landscape. Birds eat impressive quantities of insects. To attract them, plant bushes with red berries such as mountain ash, holly, and cotoneaster.

One of the most effective ways to ensure a healthy lawn and garden is to keep it clean.

Gardener's Tip

Save money by applying pest controls at the right time. For instance, don't spray when it is raining or windy or when the sun is bright. You waste both effort and the cost of the spray, because you will soon have to repeat the procedure.

Recycle and Save

There's no need to run out and buy everything you need. Frugal gardeners look for ways to use what they have or what they can find at minimum cost. Sometimes you'll find that recycled items, imaginatively used, are actually more distinctive and effective than high-cost materials purchased new.

■ Look for planters that cost little or no money. For example, a small, discarded water heater cut in half provides the basics for a planter. Drill holes for drainage, paint the outside, and fill with colorful annuals.

■ Wooden crates or boxes of any kind make good planters. Clean them up with sandpaper, but leave them a little rough for a pleasant, natural look. Treat them with a coat of stain, if desired, or allow them to weather naturally.

■ Group quart-size wooden strawberry boxes for a charming set of small, matching planters.

■ An old wheelbarrow or child's wagon, even one in disrepair, can be made into a whimsical container for plants or other garden decorations. Spruce it up a little, but don't try to make it look like new. Fill with geraniums for the summer; replant with chrysanthemums in the fall. Pile in pumpkins to celebrate the harvest.

■ An old-time watering can makes a delightful planter. If you're lucky you may find one at a garage sale for a few dollars. Don't worry if it leaks—planters need drainage holes anyway.

■ Purchase an inexpensive imported tin watering can. Plant perky mums or pansies in a pot and set it inside the can. Settle it on a front step.

■ Empty gallon metal paint cans make good planters. Want color? No problem. Coat with a primer, then paint the can.

■ Don't throw away those battered or burned-out stew pots. Put them to use holding plants.

■ Do you have an old wooden chair, too far gone to use in the dining room? Brighten it with paint in a cheerful color. Mass a few containers of flowers around it, and position a low pot on its seat.

Create interesting focal points with antique ornaments.

■ Don't let a stump in your yard stump you. Put it to work as a site for a birdhouse or a pot of geraniums.

■ Ask local potters if they sell seconds. You may be able to save as much as 50 percent on cracked, smudged, or irregular pots, perfectly adequate for outdoor container planting.

■ The long, narrow water holders sold to moisten preglued wallpaper make great planters, especially for vegetable seedlings, such as tomatoes. Available in black and white, they cost only a dollar or two. Use an ice or lobster pick to punch drain holes in the bottom. These inexpensive planters can be reused for several seasons.

■ For a contemporary planter, use a chimney liner.

■ Use a shallow metal or plastic dish as a birdbath. Elevate it on a fence post or length of log anchored in the ground.

■ Make a scarecrow to watch over the garden from a few pieces of wood and some old clothing. Stuff the clothing with straw, and tie the legs of the pants and the arms of the shirt to keep the straw in place. Make a face, or attach a hat at a rakish angle to the center pole.

■ Use cheap blinds to screen your trash cans, or as a privacy screen around your patio.

More Recycle and Save

■ Make decorative garden signs from scrap wood. Use them to mark herbs, flowers, even bushes. Note as much or as little information as you like. Or try your hand at a larger sign embellished with philosophical gardening advice. Use odds and ends of leftover paint, which holds up better than outdoor varnish.

■ Create a gate, even if you don't have a fence. Sink posts and attach a recycled garden gate. Grow shrubs or hedges on each side if you wish.

■ Fasten unused shutters together to create a screen for trash cans. Leave old shutters in a distressed state or repaint.

■ Use old volleyball netting to cover berry bushes.

■ Cut bottoms and tops off cans and use to protect tomato, pepper, and eggplant seedlings from cutworms.

■ Paper-towel and toilet-tissue tubes also make good cutworm collars. Placed around the stems of young transplants, the cardboard protects the tender stems from

Give an old mailbox a fresh coat of paint and place it near your garden as a storage place for your garden notebook and supplies. Let an annual climbing vine like morning glories or pole beans ramble up its support.

damage. As the plants mature and become too tough to be of interest to insects, the cardboard gradually decays.

■ Wire old screens together to make A-frame protectors to keep rabbits or other small animals from feasting on your tender shrubs.

■ Turn unused storm windows into a simple cold frame for

Lawn chairs with a fresh coat of paint brighten this brick patio edged with containers of impatiens, geraniums, and begonias.

hardening the plants you start from seed. Build the frame's sides from scrap wood, making the back higher than the front. Fasten the windows to the back edge with hinges so that you can set them ajar on warm, sunny days.

■ Fashion a hose holder from a piece of scrap wood. Set three wooden pegs in a triangular pattern on an 8-x-18-inch piece of wood. Attach it to the side of the building near the water faucet. Drape the hose around it to keep it out of the way. Make several if you have more than one hose.

Choosing and Caring for Equipment

Whatever you hope to accomplish with your landscaping, the proper equipment helps you reach your goals with less work and more pleasure.

Spending Wisely on Tools

The proper tools make the hard work of gardening easier and in the end save time and frustration, as well as money. When you go shopping for tools, expect to see so many that you have a difficult time choosing.

Decide what you need before you shop. Don't buy something just because it's on sale.

Seek advice. Ask the salesclerk to demonstrate equipment. Talk to friends and neighbors about their tools and why they like or dislike them.

Spend a little more for better quality. Two inferior tools cost more than one good one: If you have to replace a cheap tool after a year or two of use, you have wasted money. Invest wisely, be patient, and buy only the essentials at first. You can add to your collection in the future.

When you buy new tools look them over carefully:

- Try out different sizes.
- Compare quality.
- Handle them and see how they feel in your hands.
- Try out both short and long handles to see which you prefer.

Other qualities to consider include weight and strength. Weight plays a big factor in which tools to buy. Although you want a good solid tool, an afternoon spent using an especially heavy hoe will tire you out more than one spent with a properly sized and weighted tool.

Make sure metal parts have strength. You don't want to put your shovel in the ground a few times, then see your bargain bend. Nor do you want the tines on rakes to bend easily.

Save money by buying good tools secondhand at garage sales. Often

Gardener's Tip

Gardeners spend a lot of time on their knees. Use a purchased kneeler or improvise one by placing a piece of foam rubber in a plastic bag.

Look for good-quality used tools at garage sales.

you can find excellent-quality old tools that need some simple sprucing up. Examine used tools carefully. Avoid those with

- Loose fittings
- Split handles
- Rust and pitting on metal parts
- Broken or bent tines on rakes and pitchforks.

Gardener's Tip

Clean old tools with steel wool and rub them with oil. Sharpen blades. Sand rough handles.

Begin with the Basics

Use these descriptions to draw up a list of tools you think will meet your needs, then prioritize your purchases.

Shovels and forks. A good garden spade is indispensable. You will use it over and over for digging holes when you are planting or prying stones from garden beds. Try out different styles — long and short handles, D-shape grips, and so on. A garden fork is equally handy, but its uses are different. It makes it easier to turn over garden soil and to turn your compost pile occasionally.

Rakes. Buy at least two rakes. For raking leaves and grass clippings, you will find plastic, bamboo, and metal versions in a variety of widths. For raking gardens, leveling seedbeds, and breaking up clumps of dirt, you need a rake with short, sturdy metal tines set at a right angle to the handle. Notice the weight and length of the handle.

Hoes and cultivators also come in various sizes and styles. Hoes may have blades from 2½ to 8 inches wide, in both shallow and deep styles. You'll find that certain hoes work best in specific situations. If you use a hoe mainly to cut off weeds, look for one light enough to wield for a period of time. Cultivators, with their prongs, allow you to get close to plants to loosen the soil and rout weeds. Test both long- and short-handled versions.

Wheelbarrow. A wheelbarrow or other wheeled garden cart is essential for moving around soil, plants, rocks, tools, and other equipment. It also carries garden refuse and heavy bags of fertilizer and grass seed, and provides a good place to mix potting soil or cement. Push around a variety of wheelbarrows to see which kind suits you. For its stability, you may prefer a four-wheeled cart to a three-wheeled barrow. Try out both metal and plastic wheelbarrows. Plastic often costs less, and is lighter and easier to push. Avoid a barrow that is flimsy, though, or you'll be replacing it before many years of use.

Hand tools. Trowels come in different sizes and shapes. Their tapered metal ends are useful when planting flowers, bulbs, and small woody plants. Look for narrow styles as well as more standard 3- or 4-inch-wide blades. A hand cultivator is useful for breaking up soil and dislodging weeds.

Test new tools to be sure you like their weight, length, and balance.

Shears and pruners. You may eventually want three different kinds. Garden shears are useful for removing faded flowers or diseased leaves. (You may find that all-purpose kitchen shears work as well.) You also will need garden pruners for heavier duty; keep them sharpened to make pruning jobs easier. Use sturdy, long-handled pruners to weed out high limbs in trees.

Grass clippers or edgers ease the chore of finishing along garden beds, paths, and driveways. Look for smooth action and sharp blades.

Hedge clippers have long, scissorlike blades useful for trimming hedges and for cutting

down perennials that have finished blooming.

Carriers. You'll need something to hold clippings, weeds, and cut flowers. Recycled buckets, pails, and baskets with handles all work well. An all-purpose tarpaulin or old blanket is useful when you are raking leaves in the fall. Spread it out on the lawn, rake all of your leaves and twigs onto it, then gather up the four corners and carry or drag the whole thing to the compost pile.

Other tools. If your lawn is sizable, you may want a small spreader to apply grass seed and fertilizer. Try to buy on sale.

Taking Care of Your Investment

Proper storage and maintenance will keep tools in good condition for years.

Always store tools and landscaping equipment out of the weather. If you don't have shed, basement, or garage space for storage, protect equipment with a waterproof cover. Plan to add space for storage as soon as finances allow.

Paint the wooden handles of tools a bright color so that they are easy to spot if left lying in the garden or on the grass. This will help you find them and put them away.

Gardener's Tip

Before you work on any power mower, disconnect the spark-plug wire to avoid an accidental ignition. If you tilt the mower to examine the underside, do not do it over grass or near other plantings, which could be damaged if you spill gasoline.

Keep tools clean. Rust is the worst enemy of metal tools. Scrape dirt off metal parts after use. Keep a bucketful of sand that is saturated with oil near your tool-storage area. Run the tool up and down through the sand to both polish and oil it before putting it away.

At the end of the season, clean metal parts with kerosene to remove grease, caked oil, and dirt. Swab with oil (a good way to recycle used automobile oil) before storing.

This is also a good time to repair, repaint, or sharpen your tools. To sharpen, use a file or whetstone and take care not to cut yourself.

Practice preventive maintenance, especially on mowers, both hand mowers and riding mowers. You'll save money on repairs and add years to the life of your mower. Clean your mower, too, before storing it. At the same time, do the following maintenance check:

■ Remove and sharpen the blade (or have it sharpened).

Practice preventive maintenance on all of your tools and equipment to keep them in good working order.

- Scrape or wire-brush any accumulation of grass under the mower with a stiff brush.
- Change the oil.
- Remove the air filter and clean or replace, if needed.
- Check the muffler for signs of wear. Replace if necessary.
- Oil the bearings if dry.
- Clean all terminals and connecting cables.
- Clean the body of the mower. Sand, file, or steel-wool off any rust spots. Touch up where needed. Apply a coat of wax.
- For riding mowers, remove the battery before storing the machine and check the air pressure of pneumatic tires.

Final Touches to Your Landscape

*W*alkways and fencing define the landscape. Fencing serves a variety of purposes: it sets a style, increases safety, provides privacy, and marks property lines. Walkways increase accessibility to different parts of the yard, save plantings from traffic, and delineate spaces.

Walkways for Free—or Almost Free

Simple trail. One of the most inviting walkways is a trail through the woods—a simple dirt path. If your soil drains well, this may work in your yard as well. To improve drainage and avoid having the path turn to mud in rainy weather, dig down a few inches along the course of the pathway and spread a layer of gravel; replace soil. Top the soil with a layer of shredded or chipped wood. Keep the path neat by raking wandering pieces of wood back onto it occasionally.

Wood slabs. Saw oversize logs (10 inches or more in diameter) across the grain into thick slabs to form unevenly round steps. To inhibit decay, treat with a preservative. Settle the wood slabs in place, and fill between the cracks with sand. Space them a comfortable step apart.

Make wider steps of old timbers or railroad ties settled into the ground. These are especially useful on inclines. Again, give them more stability by filling around them with sand.

Paving stone is a more expensive walkway material. Look for a dealer who sells broken, outsize, or undersize pieces (like bluestone or slate). Collect stones yourself to save even more money.

Make pavers. Save dollars by making concrete pavers with premixed, bagged concrete. Once you set up a work area, you can get quite an assembly line going. Add some color to the concrete if you like. You don't have to limit yourself to oblongs or squares. Make two or three free-form shapes. Alternate or use them haphazardly to create the look of natural stone.

Old brick makes a delightful walk and the materials cost little. Find a contractor who has a building demolition project underway. You may be able to get used brick free if you are willing to haul it away.

Design the walk using gentle curves if you wish. Mark off the area you plan to cover, and dig it out to a depth of 6 inches. Put down 2 inches of gravel, topped by

Bark chips form a natural-looking, easy-to-maintain walkway.

2 inches of mason's sand, and rake it level. Set the bricks in a pattern, working each one into the sand. Use a carpenter's level for best results. Sweep more sand over the walk, filling between every crack. Tamp down firmly.

Gravel or crushed stone costs relatively little but makes a serviceable path. It comes in different sizes. When you order, consider mixing two different sizes for better coverage. Decide what you want, then get estimates from different sources. Make sure each bidder uses the same set of specifications.

To contain the gravel, install edging boards along the path area.

Spread the material about 2 inches deep. Level with a wide board or rake. To maintain a good-looking path, smooth it with a rake occasionally and keep it weeded. Gravel holds up well, so you can expect years of service from it.

Concrete walk. Install a concrete walk yourself. Carefully mark the location of the walk, then dig to a depth of 6 inches. Put down 2 inches of gravel for good drainage. Make your own forms for the concrete slabs. Because it's important to work quickly and efficiently once you mix the concrete, get someone to help you if possible. Mix cement according to package directions and pour it over the gravel base.

Gardener's Tip

Take your time when working on a path. Don't expect to do it all in one day. Draw a plan on paper, then lay the path out in the yard with rope or hose before beginning to dig.

Good Fences

Before you look for fencing, list the reasons you want a fence. Do you need to keep animals out or in? Do you want to safeguard your children? Do you need to provide privacy? Do you simply want to delineate your property lines?

Easy zigzag. Make a very simple zigzag split-rail fence with small trees. If you live anywhere near a logging operation, you may be able to purchase logs quite inexpensively. Eight-inch-diameter logs work well. Such a fence doesn't need perfectly straight rails. Imperfections, knots, and discolorations add to its rustic charm, and natural weathering eventually softens any defects.

Split the logs lengthwise, then again to get four rails from each tree. Lay a course of split logs in a zigzag fashion on the ground along the fence line, overlapping one over the other about 1 foot. Continue adding more courses until the fence reaches the desired height. You don't need posts: as the logs intertwine, they support each additional new level.

Picket fencing. For a simple picket fence, use a combination of pressure-treated posts and 8-foot lengths of whatever inexpensive wood is available. Borrow or rent a post-hole digger to make the holes. Sink the posts 2 feet in the ground, and space them about 7 feet apart. Don't worry about cementing them in. The fence may move a little with the frost, but it will settle again in spring. Cut each 8-foot length in

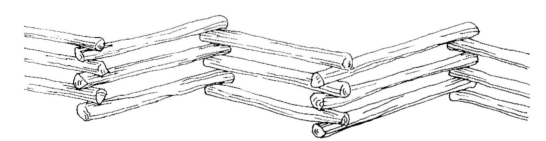

A simple zigzag fence is especially appropriate near a country or colonial-style house.

Picket fencing forms a traditional, trim-looking backdrop for a cheerful garden of salvia and impatiens, edged with ornamental grasses.

half to make the pickets. Attach 8-foot crosspieces to the posts, one at the top and one at the bottom. Nail the pickets to the crosspieces. Space pickets 2 to 2½ inches apart. Paint or stain for a weathered look.

Stockade fence. For more privacy, make a stockade-style fence. Follow the same procedure as described for picket fencing, but use longer uprights and space them closer together. You may need a third crosspiece in the middle to strengthen the fence.

Gardener's Tip

Check local zoning ordinances to find height restrictions for fencing. Some ordinances may allow only 6-foot fences, others 8-foot.

Plant a Living Fence

A row of shrubs, or hedge, has several advantages over fencing. This living fence provides texture and color to your yard, increases wind and noise protection, and lasts forever with some annual pruning, fertilizing, and mulching.

Deciduous. Lilac or forsythia "fences" have three advantages: they grow easily, they screen undesirable views, and they sport showy flowers in the spring, followed by lush green growth. If friends or relatives have these shrubs, you may be able to create this natural fencing at no cost, if you are willing to use suckers to start new plants. (See page 31 for how-tos.)

FLOWERING HEDGES
Barberry
Dogwood
Flowering quince
Forsythia
Hawthorne
Lilac
Mountain laurel
Rosa rugosa
Summersweet
Viburnum

Evergreens make a good privacy fence. Plant when they are small and keep them trimmed to encourage bushy growth. Once they reach the height you want, trim them to maintain that level. Use other hedge material, such as the popular privet, to delineate your property, too. The only disadvantage with this kind of fencing is that it needs frequent trimming to maintain the shape.

PRIVACY HEDGES
Arborvitae
Barberry
Eastern white pine
Hemlock
Holly
Juniper
Mountain laurel
Mugho pine
Norway spruce
Yew

Gardener's Tip

In northern areas, deciduous living hedges offer little privacy during the winter months.

A hedge of golden forsythia glows with color in early spring.

Index